W9-BIJ-810

This
Book
Belongs
To _

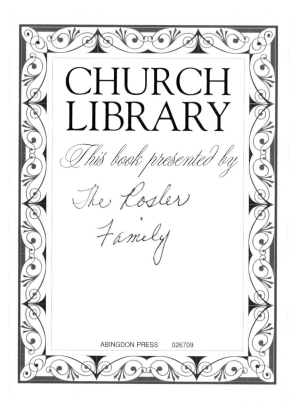

CHURCH LIBRARY

This book presented by

The Rosler

Family

ABINGDON PRESS   026709

Grolier Enterprises Inc.
SHERMAN TURNPIKE, DANBURY, CONNECTICUT 06816

Book Club Edition

An
ALICE
IN
BIBLELAND ®
Storybook

The STORY Of NOAH

Written by Alice Joyce Davidson
Illustrated by Victoria Marshall

Text copyright ©1984 by Alice Joyce Davidson
Art copyright ©1984 by The C.R. Gibson Company
Published by The C.R. Gibson Company
Norwalk, Connecticut 06856
Printed in the United States of America
ISBN 0-8378-5067-3
D.L. TO: 202-1988

Alice just loved animals.
She had a dog and kitten,
And fed a little sparrow
That nested in a mitten.

At Bible School Alice liked to read
How Noah heard God's words
And built an ark and filled it up
With animals and birds.

One rainy day she held a book
Of Bible stories on her lap.
She was reading about Noah
When she heard a rap-tap-tap.

Through her window Alice saw,
Standing on the sill,
An airmail bird who carried
This letter in his bill.

"Reading is the magic key
To take you where you want to be.
The book you're holding in your hand
Is taking you to Bibleland."

The book that Alice held became
A great big magic screen.
She walked through it to Bibleland
And came upon this scene.

She saw wicked, wicked people
Who did a lot of wrong,
And instead of singing praise to God,
They sang this awful song:

"Ha, ha, ha, he, he, he!
We're as wicked as can be!
Up with evil, down with good,
Down with love and brotherhood!
Ha, ha, ha, he, he, he!
We're as wicked as can be!"

When God saw all this wickedness,
It made Him feel quite sad.
He decided that He'd wash the earth
Of all things that were bad.

But Noah and his family
Were very, very good,
So God instructed Noah
To make an ark of wood.

03848

Noah's family built the ark,
And when the work was through,
They gathered up the animals
As God had told them to.

They took a male and female,
Just two of every kind,
The wild, the meek, the strong, the weak,
No pair was left behind.

The wicked people laughed because
There was no sea around.
Noah's ark was standing
In the middle of dry ground.

And as they laughed at Noah's ark,
God started what He planned.
A heavy rain came down and made
Big puddles on the land.

It rained and rained for forty days,
The ark floated off to sea,
And safe within it Noah sailed
With all his family.

The water covered houses,
Tall trees and mountains, too,
As God washed all things bad away
Just as He said He'd do.

After many, many months,
God made a wind blow by,
The water started going down,
The land began to dry.

Noah's ark stopped on a mountain,
Days and days went by—and then
Three times a dove searched from above
To find dry land again.

The dove flew out and back it came,
It saw no ground around.
It flew out twice—a treetop showed,
It brought a leaf it found.

The dove flew out a third time,
And this time stayed away,
So Noah and his family knew
They'd soon be on their way.

Noah and his family
Stayed in for one week more,
Then gathered all the animals
And opened up the door.

All of Noah's family
And all the animals, too,
Were happy they could stand on land
Beneath a sky of blue.

And every single creature,
Each in its very own way,
Said a special prayer to God
To thank Him for that day.

The geese honked, and the wolves howled,
Squirrels and chipmunks chattered, too.
The donkeys brayed, the horses neighed,
The two wise owls said whoooo.

The pigs said oink, the songbirds sang,
The lions roared...and then
Noah and his family
Said, "Thank You, God, Amen!"

Then God promised Noah
That He'd flood the earth no more,
And planting time and picking time
Soon would be in store.

And with love God made a rainbow
To brighten up the sky—
A reminder of His promise
As all the years go by.

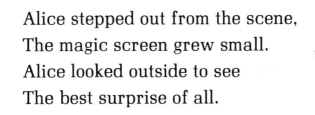

Alice stepped out from the scene,
The magic screen grew small.
Alice looked outside to see
The best surprise of all.

The rain outside was stopping,
And in the sky above
God had stretched a rainbow—
A reminder of His love.

When Alice went to Bible School,
She sang this song of praise
To thank God for His mercy,
And His tender, loving ways.

"Oh, thank you, Lord, Oh thank you,
For keeping me from harm,
For guarding me, for holding me,
Within your loving arms.

Thank you for the lessons
Of Noah and his ark,
For the rainbows after showers,
And the light that follows dark!"